BIBLE CRAFTS
ON A
SHOESTRING BUDGET

Craft Sticks & Clothespins

Rainbow Publishers®
www.rainbowpublishers.com

BIBLE CRAFTS

ON A

SHOESTRING BUDGET

Craft Sticks & Clothespins

Pamela J. Kuhn

MORE! BIBLE CRAFTS ON A SHOESTRING BUDGET: CRAFT STICKS & CLOTHESPINS
©2006 by Rainbow Publishers, seventh printing
ISBN 10: 1-58411-001-5
ISBN 13: 978-1-58411-001-9
Rainbow reorder# RB38013
church and ministry/ministry resources/children's ministry

Rainbow Publishers
P.O. Box 70130
Richmond, VA 23255
www.rainbowpublishers.com

Illustrator: Chuck Galey

Scriptures are from the *Holy Bible: New International Version* (North American Edition), ©1973, 1978, 1984 by the International Bible Society. Used by permission of Zondervan Bible Publishers.

Printed in the United States of America

Table of Contents

Memory Verse Index

Introduction

Do your students enjoy making crafts? No doubt! Next question: Are you looking for crafts that are fun and inexpensive? *Bible Crafts on a Shoestring Budget* is your answer. Based on everyday items like craft sticks and clothespins, these crafts are designed to get kids excited about the Lord. And with the reproducible patterns and easy instructions, you can focus your energy on teaching the Bible.

Each chapter begins with a Bible story, which is matched with a memory verse and discussion starters. After you tell the story, there are two craft projects that will help students retain the lesson's message and learn the memory verse.

This book is intended to make class time enjoyable for the teacher, too. Each craft includes:

What You Need: a materials list

Before Class: ideas for pre-craft preparation

What to Do: a step-by-step guide to completing the craft

What to Say: talking points to help you relate the lesson

Adapt these lessons to fit your Sunday school or vacation Bible school students. Use them in your Christian day school art classes or in your home. You will be reinforcing Scripture and stories from the Bible — the greatest book ever written — and creatively making a permanent impression on the hearts of your children.

Self-worth

Memory Verse

For great is his love toward us.
~Psalm 117:2

One Special Lamb
Based on Luke 15:1-7

The Pharisees, who strictly obeyed the Jewish law, were not happy with Jesus. "This man eats with sinners," one of them muttered.

"He is friends with law-breakers and tax collectors," complained another.

Jesus was aware of their muttering and anger. But He had not just come for the rich, the good and the handsome. "I have come for everyone," Jesus said to the Pharisees. Then Jesus told a story, comparing God to a shepherd.

"A shepherd was out on the hillside, watching his sheep. He found them good grass to eat and led them to a stream of still water so they could drink. All day, he watched his sheep. Soon it was night and time for the sheep to be in the fold.

"The sheep went in one by one as the shepherd counted. One, two, three…55, 56, 57…83, 84, 85…97, 98, 99. The shepherd looked around. Where was the last sheep? He had 100 sheep. But it was nowhere to be found.

"The shepherd shook his head. What was he going to do? *I can't leave the poor thing out all alone*, he thought. *A lion or a bear could get it. It could be hurt even now.*

"So closing the gate of the sheep fold, the tired shepherd went out to look for the lost sheep. Then he heard a small noise, 'Baaa, baaa,' he heard.

" 'I'm coming, I'm coming,' " the shepherd called. The shepherd looked over the rocks and saw the sheep caught in a thorn bush. He reached out his staff and caught the sheep by the neck, pulling him to safety.

" 'Baa,' the sheep complained.

" 'I know, little sheep. I'll have you warm and back in the fold before you know it. I'll put some ointment on the places where the thorns jabbed you.'

"The shepherd was so happy over finding the lost sheep. He walked as fast as he could. Opening the door of the fold the shepherd said, 'Look, I have found the sheep that was lost!' "

Jesus looked at the Pharisees and said, "Just like the one sheep was valuable to the shepherd, so all these are valuable to Me. They are all equally as important. There will be more rejoicing in heaven over one of these who are saved than over 99 who think they will get to heaven because they are better than anyone else."

For Discussion

1. How important are you to God?

2. Are you as important as your friend sitting beside you? Why or why not?

I'm Special, Too

This craft time will allow the children to feel how special they are.

What You Need

⇨ dolls and verse from page 11

⇨ clothespins

⇨ magnets

⇨ glue

⇨ crayons

⇨ wiggle eyes

Before Class

Duplicate the boys and girls from page 11 for each child. Cut out the boys and girls. Write each child's name on the appropriate gender of doll. Make one for yourself, too.

What To Do

1. Mix up the dolls and give each child one. Make sure no one gets a doll with his or her own name on it.

2. Instruct the children to write a word on the line that describes the one whose name they chose (for example: kind, brave, helpful, friendly, happy, etc.).

3. Allow the children to color the doll.

4. Instruct the children to glue the doll to the clothespin and glue a magnet to the back.

5. Instruct the children to cut out the memory verse and clip it to the clothespin.

6. Give the completed doll to the appropriate child.

SAY

What did your friend say about you? (Allow time for the children to respond.)
You are special to all your friends, but even more to God. Let's say the memory verse.

is

is

For great is his
love toward us.

Psalm 117:2

Into the Fold

Making and playing this game will remind your students how special they are to God.

What You Need

⇨ duplicated lambs from page 13

⇨ craft sticks

⇨ glue

⇨ scissors

⇨ cotton balls

⇨ two large canning jars

⇨ brown construction paper

⇨ tape

Before Class

Duplicate the lambs from page 13 for each child. Wrap brown paper around the canning jars and tape it in place.

What To Do

1. Allow the children to cut out the lambs.

2. Instruct them to glue the lambs to the craft sticks.

3. Have the children glue cotton balls to the lambs.

SAY

Remember how the shepherd was eager to get all his lambs in the fold? We're going to divide into teams and see whose fold is the fullest. Just like the lambs were special to the shepherd, you are special to God. He wants to make sure you make it to the fold of heaven.

Game Rules

1. Divide the class into two teams.

2. Each member should stand over the jar, holding his or her lambs at waist height. Each team should try to see how many lambs they can get into the fold (the jars) by dropping the lamb from waist level .

3. Add the points and see which team wins.

12

Thanksgiving

Memory Verse

Give thanks to the Lord...tell of all his wondrous acts. ~1 Chronicles 16:8-9

Just One Remembered
Based on Luke 17:12-19

As Jesus was walking through a village, 10 lepers were waiting for Him. They had heard that Jesus was coming that way. They had agreed together that they would ask Him to heal them.

The lepers weren't allowed on the road. They weren't allowed to be around their families or other people that they loved. Lepers wore hoods over their heads and scarves across their eyes to cover up the ugly sores caused by the leprosy.

"Jesus," they cried when they saw Him coming. "Jesus, please heal us."

Many of the lepers had tears in their eyes. They were so tired of living alone. They missed their families, they missed the village and the temple. "Have mercy on us, Jesus," they begged.

Jesus stopped in front of them. "Go," He said, "show yourselves to the priests."

The lepers were overjoyed. They knew this was Jesus' way of saying, "You are healed." Only those who had been healed were allowed to go to the priests.

The lepers couldn't wait to be declared clean. Running, they hurried to the priests. They looked at their skin and saw healthy skin.

Suddenly, one man stopped. *I forgot to say, "thank You,"* he thought. Turning around he ran back to Jesus. He bowed down in front of Jesus and said, "Thank You, thank You, thank You! Thank You for healing me of my leprosy."

Jesus looked around. "But didn't I heal ten?" He asked. "Where are the other nine?"

The man shook his head. "I don't know, I just wanted to thank You for what You did for me."

Jesus smiled. "You can go, it was your faith that made you well. Your thankfulness has made Me glad."

For Discussion

1. Has God ever answered one of your prayers?

2. Did you remember to thank Him for the answer?

Streamers of Praise

These Streamers of Praise are easy to make, but they will encourage your students to remember the things for which they should praise the Lord.

What You Need

- ⇨ hearts from page 16
- ⇨ pink paper
- ⇨ spring-type clothespins
- ⇨ crepe paper streamers or ribbon
- ⇨ scissors
- ⇨ glue
- ⇨ markers

Before Class

Duplicate the hearts from page 16 on pink paper for each child. Cut the crepe paper or ribbon into three 18" pieces per child. Make a sample craft so you can participate in the time of praise.

What To Do

1. Give each child the duplicated hearts to cut out.
2. Instruct the children to write what they are thankful for on the hearts.
3. Allow them to glue the hearts to the ends of the streamers.
4. Demonstrate how to clip the streamers in the clothespins.
5. Instruct the children to write, "Thank You, Jesus" on the clothespin.
6. Instruct the children to form a circle. Sing the praise song below (or any praise songs) together while waving the Praise Streamers. Allow each child to add in the song one thing from the streamer hearts for which they are praising the Lord.

I Praise You (Tune: "Farmer in the Dell")

I praise You for my mom,
I praise You for my mom,
You are worthy of my praise,
I praise You for my mom.

I would like to thank the Lord for you, so let's sing "I praise You for my class." Then each of you can choose something for which to praise the Lord. Remember our memory verse? (Allow the children to repeat it with you.) "Give thanks to the Lord...tell of all His wondrous acts." When we sing our praise wc are telling each other what Jesus has done for us.

Thankfulness Flowers

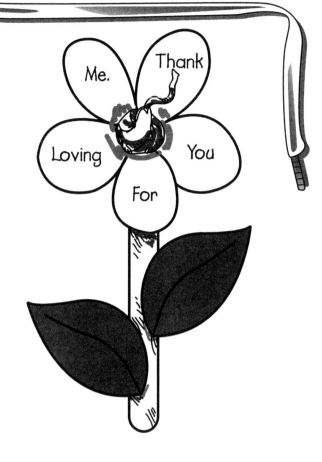

Making these Thanksgiving Flowers will promote a thankfulness in your students for the kind deeds others do for them.

What You Need

- ⇨ flowers from page 18
- ⇨ poster board
- ⇨ chocolate kiss candy
- ⇨ craft sticks
- ⇨ glue
- ⇨ scissors
- ⇨ markers
- ⇨ green crayons

Before Class

Duplicate the flowers and leaves on page 18 onto poster board. Make a Thankfulness Flower to give to each child. Bring extra chocolate candy for snacking.

What To Do

1. Give the flowers and leaves to the children to color and cut out.

2. Instruct the children to think of someone who has done something special for them.

3. Have the students write one word on each petal: THANK YOU FOR (then two other words, such as HELPING ME or LOVING ME).

4. Allow the children to color the craft stick green.

5. Show how to glue the flower and leaves to the craft stick.

6. Allow the children to glue the wrapped candy to the middle of the flower.

7. Instruct the children to present their flowers to the person for whom they are thankful.

SAY

When someone I love dies, I send flowers to the funeral home so the family will know I think their loved one was special. Sometimes it's good to give our flowers to people while they are still alive so they will know we think they are special. I have flowers to hand out today. (As you hand out the flowers say, "Robby, I'm thankful for you because you are polite," "Jenny, I'm thankful for you because you always help me straighten up the chairs after class," etc.)

God's Guidance

Memory Verse

The Lord will guide you always.
~Isaiah 58:11

Guided by God's Word
Based on 1 Kings 17:1-16

Elijah was staying by a brook. God was taking care of him. Twice each day, ravens would bring him food. He had the brook from which to drink.

Finally, the day came when the brook dried up because there hadn't been any rain. *What am I going to do?* he thought. *I'll just wait until God leads me. He has always guided my steps.*

God spoke to Elijah, "Go to Zarephath of Sidon and stay there. A widow will take care of you."

When Elijah arrived in the town, he saw a widow gathering sticks. Elijah greeted her and asked, "Could I please have a drink of water? I have traveled a long way."

The widow smiled and nodded. As she turned away, Elijah said, "And please bring me a piece of bread. I am hungry, too."

At this, the widow turned around. Tears stood in her eyes as she said, "I don't have any bread. I just have a handful of flour and a little oil in the bottom of the jug. I was gathering a few sticks to take home to build a fire so I can make a meal for my son and I. It will be our last meal and then we will die."

Elijah knew this was the widow God wanted to take care of him. He said, "Don't be afraid. Make me a cake of bread, then make one for you and your son. The Lord has told me that the jar of flour will not be used up and the jug of oil will not run dry until the time He sends rain."

The widow believed the words from the Lord and ran to the house, happy to obey the commands. She made a cake of bread for Elijah and took it to him. "It's true," she said excitedly. "I made your cake of bread and when I looked again the flour jug was filled and the oil jug, too."

Every day there was food for Elijah and for the woman and her son. Elijah had followed the guidance of the Lord and had not only found help himself, but he was able to help this small family.

For Discussion

1. Do you like to ask for help?

2. Have you ever been lost and had to ask for directions?

God's Word Bookmark

The children will enjoy making this bookmark to keep in their Bibles. They will be reminded of God's guidance when they read their Bibles.

What You Need

⇨ Bibles from page 21

⇨ red ribbon

⇨ scissors

⇨ glue

⇨ craft sticks

⇨ markers

Before Class

Duplicate the Bible from page 21 for each child. Cut the ribbon into one 3" length for each child. Make a sample bookmark so the children can see the finished craft.

What To Do

1. Give each child a Bible to cut out.

2. Show the children how to draw footprints with the markers by making an oval shape (foot) and five dots (toes). Instruct them to draw the footprints down the center of one side of the craft stick, leaving 2" at the top.

3. Instruct the children to glue the Bible to the top of the craft stick.

4. Show the children where to glue the ribbon in the center of the Bible.

SAY

Do you read God's Word each day? The Bible is God's way of showing you how He wants you to live. Read it for guidance.

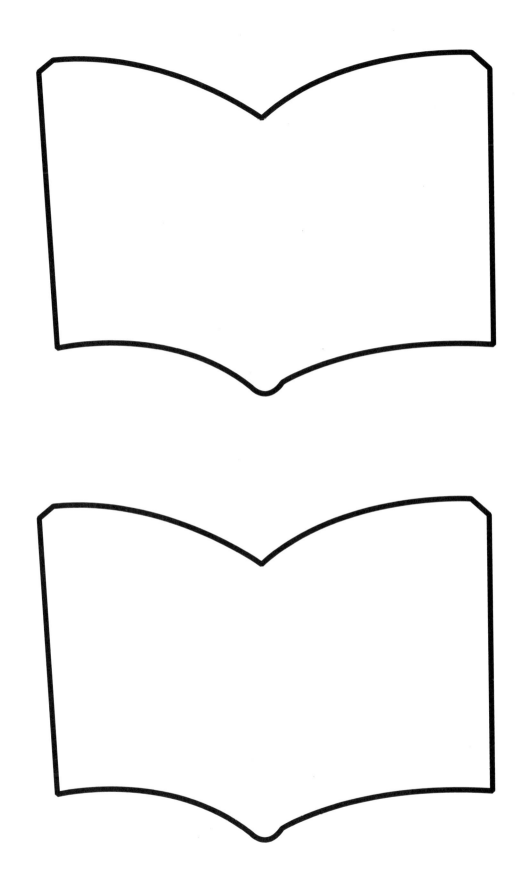

God's Word Reminder

Your students will be reminded of the guidance that they can receive from God's Word as they make and use this craft.

What You Need

⇨ reminder and verse cards from pages 23 and 24

⇨ fluorescent poster board

⇨ scissors

⇨ glue

⇨ crayons

⇨ spring-type clothespins

Remember! God's Word Will Guide You!

Revenge:
Do not seek revenge
or bear a grudge.

Leviticus 19:18

The Lord will guide you always. Isaiah 58:11

Before Class

Duplicate the reminder and the verse cards from page 23 and 24 for each child. Cut the poster board into one 4" x 6" piece for each child. Make a sample craft so the children can see the finished project.

What To Do

1. Give each child a Reminder and verse cards to color and cut out.

2. Allow the children to glue the Reminder to poster board.

3. Show the children where to glue the clothespin to the Reminder.

4. Instruct the children to clip the verse cards in the clothespin.

5. Allow the children to write on the blank card a Scripture which has helped them.

SAY

The Bible says that it is a lamp to show our feet where to go. Does it have batteries like a flashlight? What does it mean? Use these scriptures on your reminder to give you guidance.

Remember! God's Word Will Guide You!

The Lord Will Guide You Always. Isaiah 58:11

Stealing
He who has been
stealing must steal
no longer.

Ephesians 4:28

Unforgiveness
If you do not forgive men
their sins, your Father
will not forgive your sins.

Matthew 6:15

Temptation
When you are tempted,
he will also provide a
way out so that you can
stand up under it.

1 Corinthians 10:13

Revenge
Do not seek revenge
or bear a grudge.

Leviticus 19:18

Anticipation

Memory Verse
The Lord will indeed give that which is good. ~Psalm 85:12

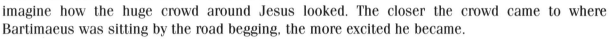

Something Great Is Going To Happen
Based on Mark 10:46-52

Bartimaeus was excited. Even though he was blind, Bartimaeus turned his eyes toward the sound of the crowd. He tried to imagine how the huge crowd around Jesus looked. The closer the crowd came to where Bartimaeus was sitting by the road begging, the more excited he became.

I just know that Jesus can heal me, Bartimaeus said to himself. *He has healed lame men so they could walk again. He healed that little boy who had an evil spirit, and He fed 5,000 people with five little loaves of bread and two fish. If He can do all that, I know He can touch my eyes and make me see.*

Bartimaeus was tired of being blind. He wanted to see the leaves he heard swaying on the trees. He wanted to see the flowers he smelled. He wanted to see the figs and grapes he ate. But most of all, Bartimaeus wanted to see this man called Jesus. He had heard so much about Jesus, he just wanted to see His kind face. Bartimaeus knew Jesus was kind because He cared so much about others.

When the crowd got a little closer, Bartimaeus cried out, "Jesus, Jesus, have mercy on me."

Those close to Bartimaeus tried to make him quiet down. "Don't bother Jesus," they said rudely.

But Bartimaeus didn't care what they said. He wanted Jesus to hear him so he cried even louder, "Jesus, have mercy on me."

Bartimaeus didn't hear Jesus say, "Call him," but he heard the others calling.

"Cheer up, Bartimaeus," one said.

"Yes," said another. "Get on your feet."

"It's Jesus. He's calling you."

Bartimaeus stood and threw his cloak he used for catching coins aside. He was led to Jesus, who asked him, "Bartimaeus, what do you want Me to do for you?"

"I want to see, Jesus," said Bartimaeus.

"Go," said Jesus. "You can see because you have believed I could heal you."

Bartimaeus looked up and his first sight was of the face of Jesus. It was a kind face. "Thank You," whispered Bartimaeus. "Thank You for healing me."

For Discussion

Do you like to look forward to a party, thinking about it for days before it finally is time?

3-D Mural

This craft will bring out the creativity of your students as they draw the background for Jesus and the blind man.

What You Need

⇨ story figures from page 27

⇨ spring-type clothespins

⇨ crayons and/or markers

⇨ glue

⇨ scissors

⇨ construction paper

⇨ white paper

Before Class

Duplicate the story figures from page 27 for each child. Cut white paper into ¾" x 3" pieces – three for each child. Make a sample mural so the children can see the finished craft.

What To Do

1. Have the children glue white paper to the center of a sheet of construction paper.

2. Give each child the story figures to color and cut out.

3. Instruct the children to draw the scene of Jesus and the blind man (suggest trees, birds, path, flowers, etc.).

4. Instruct the children to glue their strips of paper into a circle, then glue them to the back of the story figures. Allow the children to glue the figures to the mural.

5. Show the children how to glue the clothespins on either side of the back of the mural (clip side up) so that it will stand.

SAY Sometimes it's hard to imagine what it was like in Bible times. When we look at all the different murals, we can see that we all have a different idea of how it was. One thing we know for certain is that Jesus healed the blind man. Isn't He wonderful? I'm anticipating all the good things He will do for each of us.

Sunshine and Surprises

Making the sunshine, the children will imagine what it would be like to always live in darkness.

What You Need

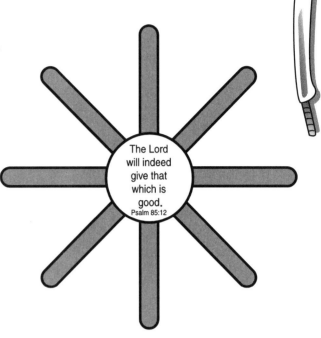

The Lord will indeed give that which is good.
Psalm 85:12

⇨ circle and chart from page 29

⇨ craft sticks

⇨ yellow and orange paint

⇨ paint brushes

⇨ small cups

⇨ scissors

⇨ glue

Before Class

Duplicate the circle and chart from page 29 for each child. Make two Xs with the craft sticks so you can demonstrate how to put the two together.

What To Do

1. Give the children four craft sticks. Instruct them to paint two yellow and two orange.

2. While the sticks are drying, allow the children to color and cut out the circles and chart.

3. Demonstrate how to glue the two yellow sticks in an X-shape. Instruct the students to glue the orange sticks the same way.

4. Instruct the children to glue the verse circle in the center of the sun.

SAY

Can we anticipate something special will happen every day? The blind man saw the sun for the first time. Look around you each day and know the Lord gives good things to us. What can you see if you look around? (Allow time for student response.) Find something special each day, write it down and bring your paper back next week so we can share your joy.

> The Lord
> will indeed
> give that
> which is
> good.
> Psalm 85:12

Special Surprises for _____	
Monday	
Tuesday	
Wednesday	
Thursday	
Friday	
Saturday	

Forgiveness

If you do not forgive men their sins,
your Father will not forgive your sins.
~Matthew 6:15

Forgiven But Not Forgiving
Based on Matthew 18:21-335.

This is a story Jesus told to teach His disciples about forgiveness.

There was a king who loved his servants. He tried to do good things for them. Among the things the king did was to lend them large sums of money.

When the day came that the accounts were to be settled, a servant who owed a lot of money came before the king. "My debt is so large," he said "I cannot hope to repay it."

The king was surprised. The servant knew this was the day to settle the debts. "I'll take all your possessions then sell you, your wife and your children for slaves," the king said.

The servant fell to his knees. "Oh, King, have mercy on me. Just a little more time," he begged. "I'll find a way to pay you back."

The king felt sorry for the servant. "Arise, go home to your wife and children. I will cancel the debt and you won't have to pay it back."

The servant was so excited! He began walking toward home, happy for the huge debt that was paid. Then he noticed a man who owed him money walking ahead of him. He grabbed the man roughly and said, "You owe me money. Pay it now."

"B-b-but I can't," said the man. "Have mercy on me, please. I will pay you as soon as I am able."

But the servant wouldn't listen. He had the man thrown into prison. "I'll get you out when I get my money," he told the man.

When the king found out how unforgiving the servant had been, he called for him again. "I showed mercy to you," said the king. "Why didn't you have mercy on someone who owed you only a portion of what you owed to me? Guards, take him away to jail."

Jesus told His disciples, "Unless you are willing to forgive those who have wronged you, God will not forgive you."

For Discussion

1. Do you like to be forgiven when you hurt someone, or if you forgot to do your chores?

2. How easy is it for you to forgive others?

Gone Forever Game

Making and playing the Gone Forever Game will teach your children the beauty of forgiven and forgotten sins.

What You Need

⇨ hearts from page 32

⇨ craft sticks

⇨ blue construction paper

⇨ two large coffee cans

⇨ glue

⇨ small juice cans

Before Class

Duplicate the hearts from page 32 for each child. Glue construction paper to the coffee cans to make them look like a sea. Make a set of game pieces in case you need to be on a team.

What To Do

1. Give each child a set of hearts to cut out.

2. Instruct the children to glue the hearts to the ends of craft sticks.

3. Allow the children to glue the blue construction paper to juice cans so they can play the game at home.

4. To play the game: Divide the class into two teams. Place the cans two feet away from the teams. Each team member has five chances to drop the sins into the sea. The team with the most points in the can wins.

SAY

God has promised that when He forgives our sins He puts them in the sea and never remembers them again. We have to do our part, though, by asking Him to forgive our sins. Just like some of the sins didn't go into the can, our sins that we don't confess to God aren't buried in the sea. They will remain unforgiven.

Stealing
1 point

Disobedience
2 points

Lying
3 points

Disrespect
4 points

Selfishness
5 points

The King's Scroll

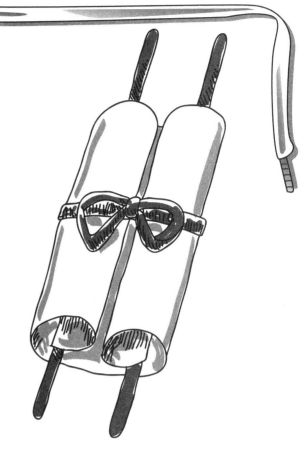

Making this scroll will remind the children they can have their sins forgiven...and forgotten!

What You Need

⇨ verse from page 34

⇨ crayons

⇨ scissors

⇨ glue

⇨ craft sticks

⇨ ribbon

Before Class

Duplicate the verse from page 34 for each child. You can also use it in telling the Bible story. Read the "loan" from it, then write "forgiven" across it.

What To Do

1. Allow the children to color and cut out the verse.

2. Instruct the children to glue a craft stick to the short ends of the scroll.

3. Demonstrate how to roll the ends toward the middle to make a scroll.

4. Practice repeating the verse while the children use their scrolls.

5. Give each child a piece of ribbon to tie around the scroll.

SAY

When we ask God to forgive our sins, He writes "forgiven" on them. When God forgives us, He blots our sins out and He no longer remembers them. Have you been forgiven?

If you do not forgive men their sins,
your Father will not forgive your sins.

Matthew 6:15

Promises
. . . .

I Promise
Based on Ruth 1
. . . .

Naomi lived in Moab. She and her husband and sons moved there because of the famine in their own country. Then her husband and two sons died. Naomi decided to return home to Bethlehem.

Naomi told her daughters-in-law, Ruth and Orpah, her plans. "I have lost my husband and sons and want to go back to my home. You must go back to the homes of your fathers," urged Naomi. "You will find another husband worthy of you."

"Let us go with you," the women begged.

"No, I am an old woman. You should stay in Moab where you belong."

Orpah agreed to do as Naomi asked, but Ruth loved Naomi and wouldn't leave her. Ruth promised, "I will take care of you. Where you go, I will go. Where you make your home, I will make my home. Your people will be my people and the God you serve will be my God."

Together, Naomi and Ruth journeyed to Bethlehem. The 50 miles seemed long and they were relieved to reach their new home. Ruth kept her promise. She had gone where Naomi went. She made her home where Naomi was making her home.

"How will we eat?" asked Naomi.

"You have told me many times about how those harvesting the grain leave extras in the field for the poor," said Ruth. "Tomorrow I will go and gather grain."

Naomi sighed. "I wish you didn't have to work so hard, Ruth."

"I don't mind. I promised to take care of you. And your God who is my God will provide, just as He promised."

Ruth and Naomi were surprised how God kept His promise. Ruth went to gather grain in the fields of Boaz. Boaz was impressed with Ruth's devotion to her mother-in-law. Soon, Ruth and Boaz were married. How happy Naomi was when Ruth gave birth to a son!

Ruth had promised many things to her mother-in-law. She kept each one and added even more blessings to the ones she gave to Naomi. Obed, Ruth's son, brought Naomi much happiness. She was glad Ruth had come to Bethlehem with her.

For Discussion

Has anyone ever made a promise to you but didn't keep it? How did that make you feel?

Compass Spinner

Making the Compass Spinner will remind your students that promising to go with Jesus is the best way!

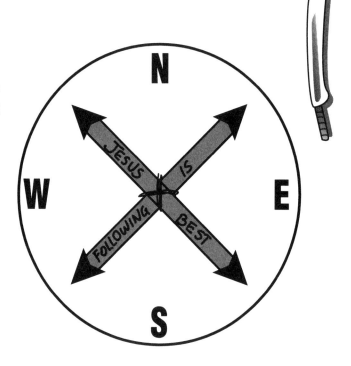

What You Need

⇨ compass and arrows from page 37

⇨ craft sticks

⇨ glue

⇨ crayons

⇨ scissors

⇨ fishing line

⇨ thin-line markers

Before Class

Duplicate the compass and arrows from page 37 for each child. Make a sample spinner and hang it in the doorway of your classroom.

What To Do

1. Give each child a compass and four arrows to color and cut out.

2. Instruct the children to glue two craft sticks together to form an X.

3. Instruct the children to glue an arrow on the end of each craft stick.

4. Help the students tie fishing line around one craft stick, close to the center.

5. Show how to glue the craft sticks to the center of the compass.

6. Assist the children in printing "Following Jesus Is Best" on the craft sticks (one word on each stick).

SAY

Was Ruth faithful to keep the promise she made to Naomi? If you made Jesus a promise that you will go where He wants you to go, are you going to keep your promise? (Allow time for students to respond.) Remember, north, south, east or west, following Jesus is best!

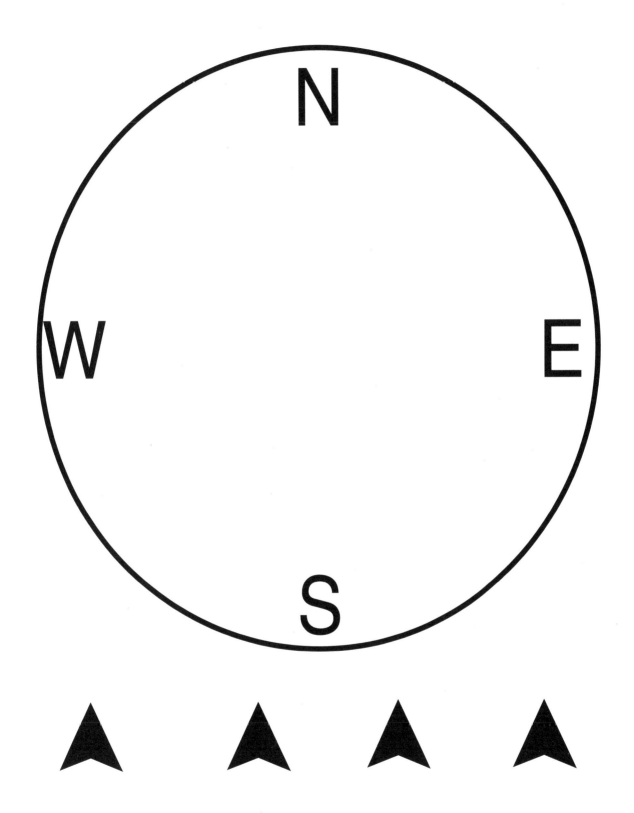

Yes or No Game

Making and playing with the Yes or No Game will reinforce to your students the importance of promise keeping.

What You Need

⇨ game board, spinner pieces and people from pages 39-40

⇨ spring-type clothespins

⇨ paper fasteners

⇨ crayons

⇨ scissors

⇨ glue

Before Class

Duplicate the game board, spinner pieces and people from pages 39 and 40 for each child. Make a sample craft to keep in the classroom for early birds.

What To Do

1. Give each child the game pieces to color and cut out.

2. Instruct the children to glue Ruth, Naomi and Boaz to the clothespins, clip up.

3. Assist the children in making the spinner by attaching the arrow with a paper fastener.

4. To play the game: Three children each choose a game piece. Using the spinner to see how many spaces to move, follow the directions on the game board.

SAY

Have you ever made a promise you didn't keep? (Allow time for discussion.) Why not? Do you think it's important to keep the promises you make? Say the verse with me and let's see what God commanded us to do.

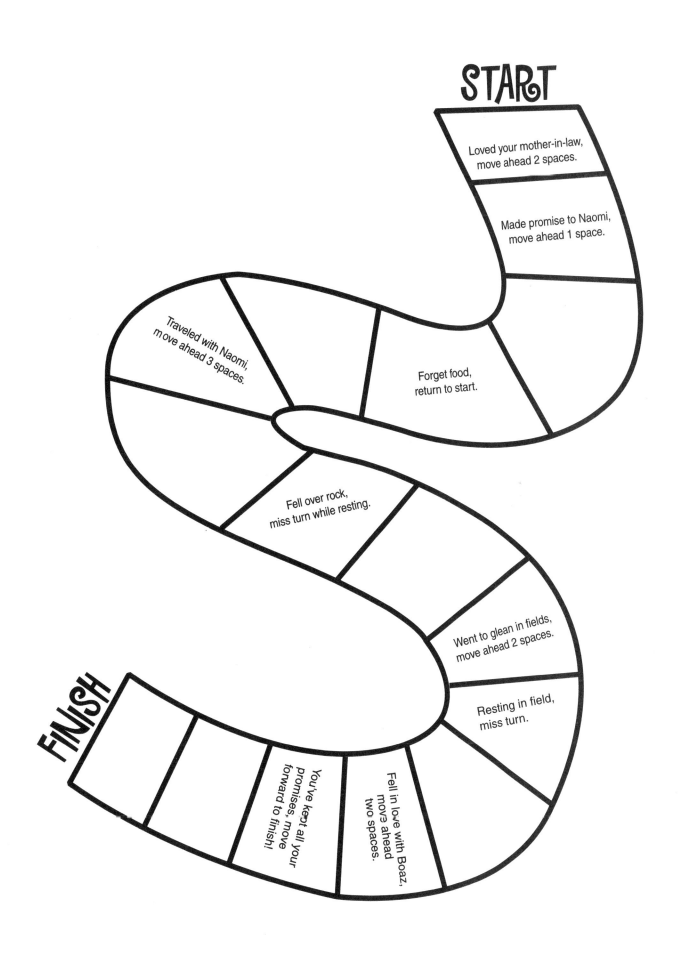

START

Loved your mother-in-law, move ahead 2 spaces.

Made promise to Naomi, move ahead 1 space.

Forget food, return to start.

Traveled with Naomi, move ahead 3 spaces.

Fell over rock, miss turn while resting.

Went to glean in fields, move ahead 2 spaces.

Resting in field, miss turn.

Fell in love with Boaz, move ahead two spaces.

You've kept all your promises, move forward to finish!

FINISH

39

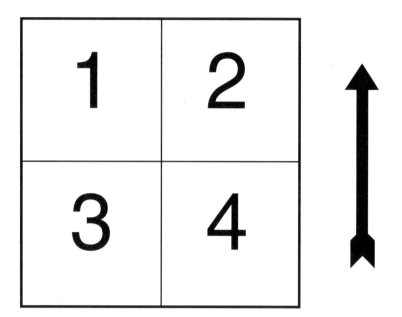

Commitment

Memory Verse

Commit your way to the Lord.
~Psalm 37:5

If I Die, I Die
Based on Esther 3-9

Esther was King Xerxes' queen. Before she married the king, Esther lived with her cousin Mordecai, who had raised her. When Esther became queen, Mordecai told her, "Don't tell anyone that you are a Jew."

King Xerxes had an official named Haman. Soon Haman became chief of all the ministers. The king made a command: "All Haman's subjects shall bow before him."

Haman enjoyed his new job. He loved seeing people bow when he walked past. But Mordecai refused to bow. He knew the command to bow only to God. Haman's frustration grew into anger and he determined to kill not only Mordecai, but all the Jewish people.

Haman wrote a decree and talked the king into putting his seal on the law. Neither the king nor Haman knew this decree meant that the queen would be killed.

As soon as the seal was on the decree, Haman sent notice to all the provinces. "On the thirteenth day of the twelfth month, all Jews, young and old, will die."

When Mordecai heard the news he sent for Esther. "Haman has plotted to kill our people. Go before the king and ask him to spare us."

Esther knew that if she went before the king without an invitation she could be killed. But she believed so strongly that the Jewish people should be saved, she said, "I will go to the king. If I die, I die."

After three days of fasting and praying, Esther dressed in her most beautiful robes. She prayed for courage as she walked toward the king's inner court.

The king was sitting on the throne. He looked up in surprise when he saw the queen. Esther bowed before him, and when she looked up she saw the golden scepter held out toward her, a sign she would not be killed.

"What request do you bring to me?" asked King Xerxes. "Whatever you ask even up to half my kingdom, I will give it to you." Queen Esther asked for the king and Haman to come to a feast.

At the feast, the king asked Esther what he could do for her.

Esther said, "My people are to be killed. I am asking you to save our lives."

The king was angry. "Who is responsible for giving this order?"

Esther pointed to Haman. "That wicked man!"

The king looked at Haman. "You will be hanged!"

Every year around the world, Jews still celebrate the holiday of Purim, the day Queen Esther was so committed to saving her people from destruction that even the threat of death didn't stop her from doing what was right.

For Discussion

1. Do you believe in something so completely that you would die before changing your mind?

2. Is your relationship with God that important to you?

41

Clothespin Story

Your children will enjoy retelling the Bible story with these clothespin people.

What You Need

⇨ story figures from page 43

⇨ spring-type clothespins

⇨ markers

⇨ scissors

⇨ glue

⇨ glitter glue pen

Before Class

Duplicate the story figures from page 43 for each child. Make a set of clothespin people to use in telling the story.

What To Do

1. Give each child a set of story figures to color and cut out.

2. Allow the children to use the glitter glue pen on the crown.

3. Instruct the children to glue the figures to the clothespins.

4. Allow the children to retell the story using their figures.

SAY

How would you feel if you were going to sneak in to see the president of the United States? (Allow time for response.) Even though Esther was queen, she wasn't permitted to come before the king without being called. She was determined to do what God wanted her to do anyway. Are you?

Mordecai

Haman

King Xerxes

Queen Esther

People

43

Queen Esther's Fan

Creating this fan will remind your students to commit their way to the Lord, just like Queen Esther.

Commit your way
to the Lord.

Psalm 37:5

What You Need

⇨ fan from page 45

⇨ markers

⇨ scissors

⇨ glue

⇨ ribbon

⇨ craft sticks

Before Class

Duplicate the fan from page 45 for each child. Make a sample fan so the children can see the finished craft.

What To Do

1. Say, "In Queen Esther's time, fans were made from ostrich feathers. The servants who fanned those in the royal court were called 'fanbearers.' "

2. Demonstrate how to glue three craft sticks in a fan shape, gluing them together at the bottom. Allow the glue to dry.

3. Give each child a fan to color and cut out.

4. Show how to glue the colored fan to the craft sticks.

5. Give each child a length of ribbon and help them tie the ribbon into a bow.

6. Show where to glue the bow on the fan handle.

SAY

As you cool yourself off, remember Queen Esther's commitment to doing what was right. Will you do what is right no matter what it may cost you?

Commit your way
to the Lord.

Psalm 37:5

45

Sharing God's Blessings...

Memory Verse

Freely you have received, freely give.
~Matthew 10:8

A Gift for Elisha
Based on 2 Kings 4

In the city of Shunem there lived a rich woman and her husband. Elisha often visited this city in his travels. The woman was always eager for Elisha to eat with them. She had her servants fix the best food they had. Elisha enjoyed the relaxing times he had visiting with them.

One day while Elisha was visiting, the woman said, "Elisha, I have made a little room for you on the roof where it is cool. This is your room whenever you need a place to stay."

Elisha was surprised. "You didn't need to give this special gift to me," he protested.

"We wanted to," the woman answered. "God has given us many things and we want to share with others."

Elisha loved his roof-top room. It was furnished with a bed, a table, a stool and a lamp. One day while Elisha was visiting there, he called one of the servants, Gehazi, to him. "What can I do for this woman who has done so much for me?" he asked.

"I have heard them talking, and she would like to have a child more than anything," Gehazi told Elisha.

Elisha called the woman to him. "Soon you will have a son," he said. Elisha's words came true and in a year she gave birth to a son.

The boy grew, but one day he became ill. His father and mother watched as their son grew weaker and weaker until he died. They were heartbroken, but remembered their friend, Elisha. Quickly the woman ran to him. "Help me, Elisha, my son is dead."

Elisha came to the boy and laid down on top of him, putting his mouth to the boy's mouth. Elisha felt the boy grow warm again. Suddenly the boy sneezed and sat up.

"Come," called Elisha. "Your boy is well."

The mother and father were overjoyed. They didn't know when they gave of their wealth to Elisha that someday he would give them their most prized possession. They received because they gave.

For Discussion

1. Do you refuse to share the good things God has given you?

2. Do you know that the more you give, the more you receive?

A Flowering Gift

This will be a fun and easy craft for your students that lets them experience the joy of giving.

What You Need

⇨ plant poke envelopes from page 48

⇨ crayons

⇨ glue

⇨ scissors

⇨ flower seeds

⇨ craft sticks

Freely you have received, freely give.
Matthew 10:8

Before Class

Duplicate the plant poke envelope from page 48 for each child. Make a sample craft so you can join the discussion of to whom you will give your gift.

What To Do

1. Give each child a plant poke envelope to color and cut out.

2. Show the children how to fold the envelopes and glue them together.

3. Allow the children to glue a craft stick to the back of the envelope.

4. Give the children seeds to put in the envelopes.

5. Explain that the Flowering Gift may be given to a friend. Say, "Tell your friend that they can plant the seeds in the packet, then poke the stick in the planter as a reminder of what the pot holds."

SAY

How has God been good to you? (Allow time for children to respond.) Do you think we should share His blessings with others? Who are you going to give your gift to? Allow time for discussion.

Freely you have
received, freely give.

Matthew 10:8

Craft Stick Bed Magnet

Freely you have received, freely give.

Matthew 10:8

Your children will enjoy making this bed for the boy who came back to life.

What You Need

⇨ boy and verse from page 50

⇨ craft sticks

⇨ scissors

⇨ glue

⇨ crayons

⇨ fabric scraps

⇨ magnet strips

⇨ cotton balls

⇨ poster board

Before Class

Duplicate the boy and verse from page 50 for each child. Cut the poster board into one 4" x 5" piece for each child. Make a sample magnet so the children can see the finished project.

What To Do

1. Give each child a boy and verse to color and cut out.

2. Give children a pre-cut sheet of poster board and instruct them to glue craft sticks to it to form a bed.

3. Instruct the children to stretch cotton balls into a pillow and glue it to the head of the bed.

4. Have the children to glue the boy to bed.

5. Instruct the students to cut a blanket from fabric to glue over the boy.

6. Instruct the children to glue the verse to the middle of the blanket.

7. Allow the students to glue a magnet strip to the back.

SAY Isn't it exciting to see how you can give joy to your friend and immediately you receive joy for yourself? The giving circle never stops. God gives love to you, you give love to your sister, your sister gives love to a friend, that friend gives love to her family…and on and on. And the whole time you receive love from others because you have given it away. Try it this week and see how it works!

Freely you have
received, freely
give.

Matthew 10:8

Freely you have
received, freely
give.

Matthew 10:8

Loyalty

Memory Verse
Do not forsake your friend.
~Proverbs 27:10

The Greatest Betrayal

Based on Mark 14:12-26, 43-44 and Matthew 27:1-10

Jesus knew Judas Iscariot was the one who would turn Him over to the enemies. It hurt Jesus to know one of His own disciples would betray Him. After Jesus had given Judas bread during the Last Supper, He said, "Go, Judas, and do what you must do."

Jesus went to Gethsemane to pray to His Father, God. He didn't want to go through the suffering He knew was coming, but He was willing if it was God's will. "Not My will," He prayed. "Let Your will be done."

Soon a commotion was heard through the trees. Jesus knew it was the time He would be betrayed by one of His closest friends. The light from torches could be seen and loud, angry voices heard.

Jesus watched the procession of priests, elders, scribes, Sadducees and Pharisees coming toward Him. Then He saw Judas at the head of the line. Jesus looked at Judas and Judas looked back defiantly.

It didn't take Judas long to come to Jesus. Loudly he said, "Hail, Master!" Then he gave Jesus a kiss on the cheek, a sign to the band of men which one was Jesus.

Judas tried to think of the 30 pieces of silver he had received for betraying Jesus. But when he saw Jesus bound and being handed over to Pilate, he was filled with sorrow.

"What have I done?" he asked himself. "I have been disloyal to the One who loved me most."

Judas took the silver back to the chief priests who had given it to him. "I have sinned. I have betrayed a sinless man."

"That's not our problem," they told Judas. "You are responsible for your own actions."

Judas threw the money into the temple and left. The pain in his heart was too much to bear. He couldn't live knowing what he had done. Judas hung himself, filled with hatred at himself for his disloyalty.

For Discussion

1. Do you have friends you stick with no matter if times are good or bad?

2. Could you be bribed to be disloyal to them?

Forever Friends Pledge

Pledging to be Forever Friends will encourage your students to treat their friends with love and care.

What You Need

➪ Forever Friends pledge from page 53

➪ markers

➪ glitter glue pens

➪ sequins

➪ spring-type clothespins

➪ glue

➪ scissors

Before Class

Duplicate the Forever Friends pledge from page 53 onto poster board. Spray paint the clothespins gold. Cut paper into one strip per child, plus one for you. Make a sample pledge so the children can see the finished project.

What To Do

1. Give each child a slip of paper on which to write his or her name. Make sure your name is included. Gather the names in a basket and allow each child to choose a name. Suggest that they keep the name they choose a secret until the end of the activity.

2. Give each child a pledge to cut out.

3. Allow the children to decorate their pledges as they wish.

4. Assist in helping the children clip their pledge to a clothespin.

5. One by one, allow the children to present their pledges to each other.

SAY

Judas wasn't a loyal friend. He stomped off to become friends with the soldiers and chief priests. Many times we get upset because a friend is playing with someone else, or not participating in the activity we chose. Don't stomp off with, "I don't want to be your friend." Instead, be a loyal friend — a Forever Friend.

I will be your
FOREVER FRIEND!

_____

Do not forsake
your friend.

Proverbs 28:10

True Blue Friends

Creating and playing this True Blue Friends game will remind your students to be loyal friends.

What You Need

⇨ envelope from page 55

⇨ blue and red paint

⇨ paint brushes

⇨ small cups for water

⇨ glue

⇨ scissors

⇨ craft sticks (4 for each child)

TRUE BLUE

Do not forsake your friend.
Proverbs 27:10

Before Class

Duplicate the envelope from page 54 for each child. Make a sample game so you can show the class how to play.

What To Do

1. Give each child an envelope to cut out. Instruct the children to paint the open letters blue.

2. Instruct the children to paint one side of their craft sticks blue. Allow to dry.

3. Assist in helping the children fold the envelopes. Help the students glue the sides.

4. Instruct the children to paint the other side of their craft sticks red.

5. Explain the game rules: Divide into two teams (more if you have a large class). Each team chooses a captain who will keep score. Each team player holds his or her sticks at waist height and drops them. Points are awarded for each blue side that is showing. The team with the most points wins.

6. The children may store their sticks in the envelope when they are finished playing.

SAY

Have you ever heard of a True Blue Friend? "True Blue" means a loyal friend. The color red is sometimes used to represent anger, probably because when someone is angry his or her face turns red! Let's play this game together and see which team is True Blue.

TRUE BLUE

Do not forsake your friend.
Proverbs 27:10

- -

God's House

Memory Verse
Let us not give up meeting together.
~Hebrews 10:25

Building Up The Temple
Based on 1 Kings 5-8

When Solomon became king, God asked him what he wanted most. "I will give you your desire," God told him.

Solomon knew he could ask for great riches. He knew he could ask for fame so everyone everywhere would know about him, the great king. Solomon knew he could ask that he would live for years and years. But there was something he wanted more.

"God, if I could have one thing, it would be wisdom so I could lead my people."

God was pleased with Solomon's answer. "Because you asked for nothing for yourself, but you were concerned with others, I will grant your wish."

Soon Solomon's wisdom was known throughout his kingdom. The people respected him and the kingdom was peaceful. Solomon decided it was time to carry out the plan of his father, David. He would build a temple to worship God.

Solomon knew about the great cedars of Lebanon, so he sent word to Hiram, the king of Tyre. "I am building a temple for God. Could I have some wood from your great cedars?"

It was quite a job. The trees had to be felled, they had to be roped to rafts and floated down the coast. While this was happening, thousands of men quarried and cut the stones for the foundation. They also cut the stones for the outer walls of the temple.

For four long years they worked to lay the foundation. Then it took three more years to build the temple. The temple was beautiful. The cedar wood had been carved with flowers and trees, then painted gold.

As the temple was being finished, it filled with a cloud. All duties stopped as the glory of God filled the temple. "Thank You, God," prayed Solomon, "that I could build this temple where others can find and worship You. There is no God like You. You have not failed to keep one of Your promises."

The king and all the people offered sacrifices to God to thank Him for this place to worship. The people went home happy and thankful for the good things God had done for them.

For Discussion

How important is church attendance to you? Are you absent if a fishing trip is offered? Do you miss when you have a ball game?

Mini Clipboards

Your students will find these Mini Clipboards fun and easy to make.

What You Need

⇨ clipboard covers from page 58

⇨ fluorescent poster board

⇨ spring-type clothespins

⇨ clear, self-stick plastic

⇨ permanent fine-tip markers

⇨ 3" x 5" paper

⇨ scissors

⇨ crayons

⇨ yarn

⇨ pencils

Before Class

Duplicate the clipboard cover from page 58 for each child. Cut the poster board into one 5" x 7" piece per child. Sharpen the pencils. Make a sample Mini Clipboard so the children can see the finished project.

What To Do

1. Give each child a clipboard cover to color and cut out.

2. Instruct the children to glue the cover to the poster board.

3. Assist the children in covering the clipboard with the self-stick plastic.

4. Allow the children to decorate a clothespin using markers.

5. Show how to glue the bottom half of the clothespin near the top of the clipboard. Allow to dry.

6. Using the clothespin, show how to clip paper to the clipboard.

7. Show how to tie a piece of yarn around the clothespin and attach the other end to a pencil.

SAY

Isn't it fun to meet with your friends and learn about God? (Listen to students' answers.) God wants us to meet together because He knows the encouragement and friendship we will receive from others who love Him, too. Use your clipboard to write down prayer requests so you can remember to pray for them all week.

I'll pray for others.

Let us not give up meeting together.
Hebrews 10:25

Our Church

The ringing of the bell will be a reminder of the importance of group worship.

What You Need

⇨ church from page 60

⇨ crayons

⇨ chenille wire

⇨ small bells

⇨ craft sticks

⇨ cardboard

⇨ scissors

⇨ glue

Before Class

Duplicate the church from page 60 for each child. Cut 5" squares of cardboard. Make a sample church so children can see finished craft.

What To Do

1. Show how to glue the craft sticks together to the back of the cardboard square in a steeple position, then glue the sticks together at the top.

2. Give each child a duplicated church. Instruct the children to color the church windows and cut the church out.

3. Instruct the children to glue their church to the square.

4. Assist in threading a chenille wire through a bell and hanging it in the craft stick steeple.

5. Demonstrate how to twist the end of the chenille wire into a loop for hanging.

SAY

Why do we come to church? (Allow time for students to respond.) How do you feel when you miss church? Worshipping with other Christians encourages us to live for Jesus. Come back next week!

Peacefulness

Memory Verse

Do not seek revenge or bear a grudge.
~Leviticus 19:18

I Could Get Even
Based on 1 Samuel 24:1-22

King Saul was jealous of David. He was glad when David killed Goliath and delivered the people from the Philistines. But then the people started singing, "Saul has killed thousands, but David has killed tens of thousands."

One day, while David was playing his harp for Saul, Saul threw his spear at David to try to kill him. David soon realized he would have to hide from the king.

David lived in the wilderness with a band of loyal followers. When Saul got word of where David was, he set out with his men to look for him.

It was a hot day and the mountains were dangerous with many rocks and cliffs. Saul was soon ready for a rest. He found a cave to sleep in, not knowing it was the same cave where David was hiding.

David waited until Saul fell asleep. "Come on," urged his men. "Kill him. He deserves to die and this is your chance."

"No," said David. "He was anointed king by God." Instead, David crept up behind Saul and cut off a piece of his robe. Quietly he waited until King Saul awoke and left the cave. Then David called out, "King Saul, see how close you came to being killed?" David held up the piece of fabric he had cut from the bottom of his robe. "If I had revenge in my heart I could have killed you. Instead, I spared your life. Can you believe that I don't mean to harm you?"

King Saul looked down at his robe. He saw the ragged edge where the robe had been cut. He knew David was close enough to kill him. "David," the king said, "You are a better man than the king. May God be with you forever."

For Discussion

1. Has someone done something to you that you've found hard to forgive?

2. Do you think of ways to get even or do you try to create peace?

Sleeping Saul Game

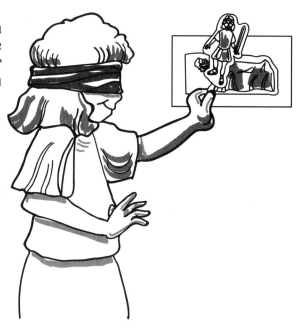

A variation of "Pin the Tail on the Donkey," the Sleeping Saul Game will be fun to play as a group and for your students to take home to play with their families.

What You Need

⇨ Saul and David figures from page 63

⇨ scissors

⇨ crayons

⇨ glue

⇨ craft sticks

⇨ sticky tack

⇨ permanent marker

⇨ blindfold

Before Class

Duplicate the Saul and David figures from page 63 for each child. Color and cut out the Saul figure to play the game in class.

What To Do

1. Give each child the Saul and David figures to color and cut out.

2. Instruct the children to glue the David figures to the top halves of two craft sticks.

3. Instruct the children to write their name on one of the craft sticks and save the other David and Saul for playing the game with a friend or brother or sister at home.

4. Put sticky tack on the back of each David that has a student's name on it. Attach sleeping Saul to the wall and play the game, blindfolding each student and seeing who can get David the closest to sleeping King Saul.

SAY

King Saul wanted to kill David. Do you think that should have made David want to kill King Saul when he found a chance to do it? (Allow time for discussion.) David knew God said, "Do not seek revenge or bear a grudge." He was willing to be peaceful.

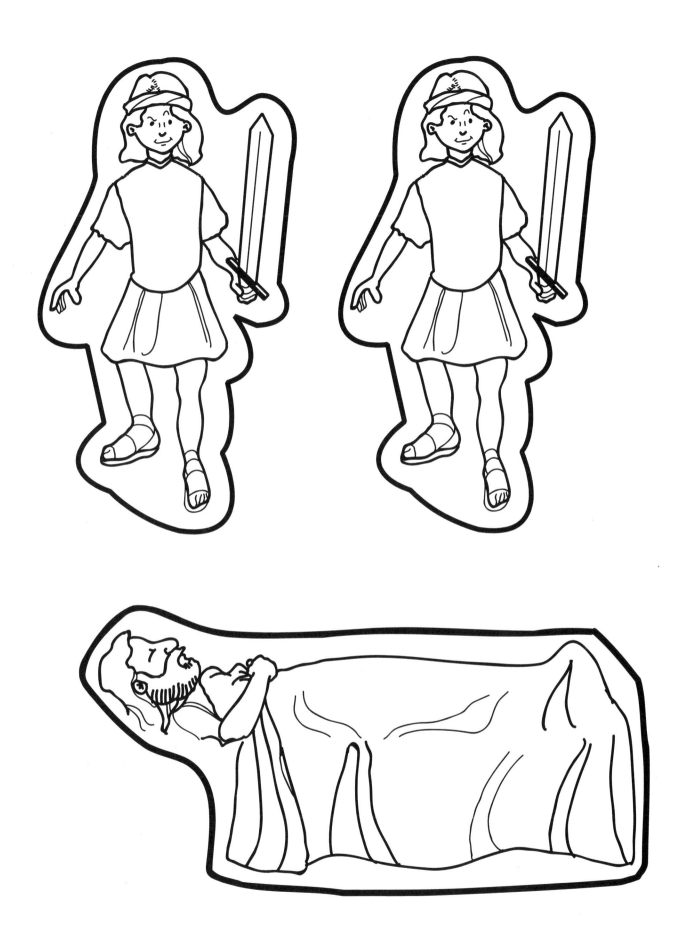

Story Puppets

By teaching King Saul the verse, the students will be reminded of David and his forgiving spirit.

What You Need

⇨ puppet pieces from page 65

⇨ craft sticks

⇨ scissors

⇨ crayons

⇨ glue

⇨ blue and purple felt

⇨ wiggle eyes

Before Class

Duplicate the puppet pieces from page 65 for each child. Using the robe pattern, cut out a purple felt robe and a blue felt robe for each student. Make sample puppets to use in telling the story.

What To Do

1. Allow the children to color and cut out the puppet pieces from page 65.

2. Show your puppets so the students can see where to glue the pieces on the craft sticks.

3. Allow the children to glue wiggle eyes on the puppets.

4. Demonstrate how to glue the finger holder pieces to form a ring on the backs of the puppets.

5. Have the children use David try to teach King Saul the verse. See if King Saul can "repeat" after David.

SAY

David had a perfect chance to seek revenge on King Saul. Did King Saul deserve whatever David would do to him? (Allow time for answers.) Let's follow David's example and not seek revenge or bear a grudge. Instead, God wants us to make peace.

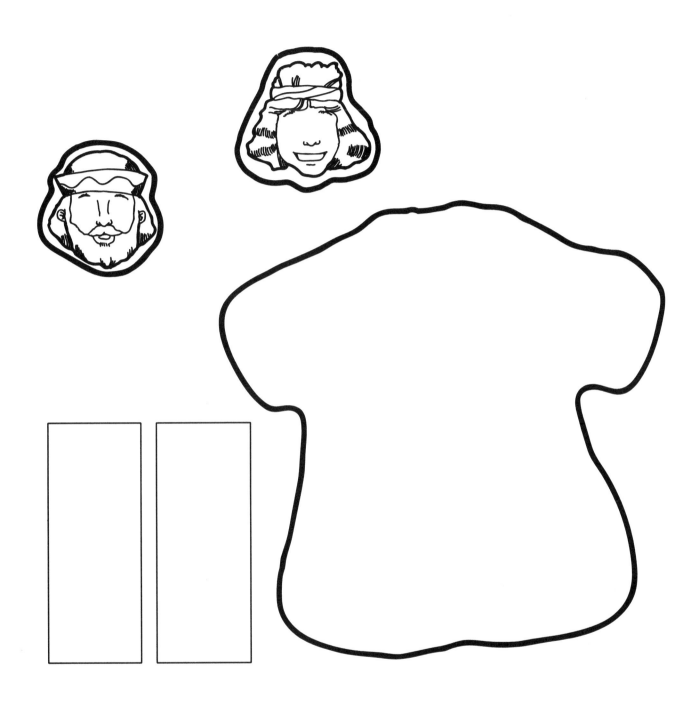

Righteousness

Memory Verse

He who has been stealing must steal no longer. ~Ephesians 4:28

Who Took It?
Based on Joshua 7:1-26

The Israelites were praising God. "Thank You, God, for the victory at Jericho" was heard throughout the camp. The tumbling walls assured the army that God was with Joshua just as He had been with Moses.

"The next city won't be any problem," said one soldier.

"Not with God's help," agreed another. "With God we are assured of the victory."

The next city was Ai. Joshua sent spies to look the town over.

"It's a small city, Joshua," reported one spy.

"We'll only need two or three thousand soldiers to capture it," said another spy.

Joshua believed the spies and sent the soldiers off to fight the men of Ai. But instead of capturing the city, the Israelites were defeated. Thirty-six soldiers were killed and the rest ran away.

"What went wrong?" Joshua asked them. "Gather the elders for prayer."

All day, Joshua and the elders prayed. "God," prayed Joshua, "all of the rest of the Canaanites have surely heard of this defeat. They will surround us and wipe us out. Did You bring us all the way back to Canaan to be destroyed?"

As the men listened for God to speak they heard, "You have been defeated because Israel has sinned. Someone has stolen some of the goods from Jericho which I said should be brought into the treasury."

It was sad to think an army was defeated because of one man's sin. Joshua knew that Israel would not be able to win the victory over their enemies until the wicked one had been punished.

"Who took it, Lord?" asked Joshua.

The thief should have known he could not hide from God. God showed Joshua who was guilty. "My son," said Joshua to Achan. "Give glory to God and tell what wicked thing you have done."

Achan hung his head. "I have taken a Babylonian coat, some silver and gold and buried it in the ground around my tent."

Joshua sent messengers to Achan's tent to dig up the stolen money and robe. "Take Achan and his sons and daughters, all his animals, his tent and all he has to the Valley of Achor," he commanded. Turning to Achan he asked, "Why have you brought this trouble on us? Today God will bring trouble on you!"

Achan and his family were stoned to death, then burned with all they owned. The children of Israel learned that God demanded obedience. Their disobedience would result in defeat.

For Discussion

1. Have you ever been tempted to take something that didn't belong to you?

2. Why is stealing wrong?

Achan's Tent

Your students will enjoy making this magnet to remind them of the memory verse.

What You Need

⇨ tent pieces from page 68

⇨ craft sticks

⇨ scissors

⇨ glue

⇨ crayons

⇨ magnet strips

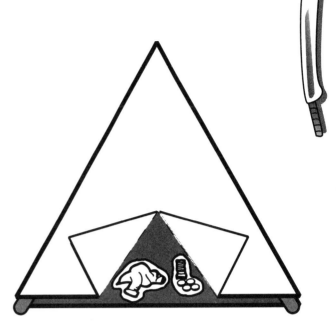

Before Class

Duplicate the tent pieces from page 68. Make a sample tent so the children can see the finished project.

What To Do

1. Give each child a set of tent pieces to color and cut out.

2. Assist the children in cutting the tent flaps and folding them open.

3. Instruct the children to glue the craft sticks on the two vertical edges of the plain tent.

4. Have the students glue the tent with flaps on top of the craft sticks.

5. Show where to glue the clothes and silver inside the open flaps.

6. Allow the children to glue a piece of magnet strip to the back of the completed tent.

SAY

When we close this tent flap, Achan's tent looks like all the others. Only God knew what Achan had hidden. Only God knows what you have hidden in your heart, too. If you have tried to hide something, why don't you talk to God about it? He's ready to forgive you! God wants to help you to be righteous.

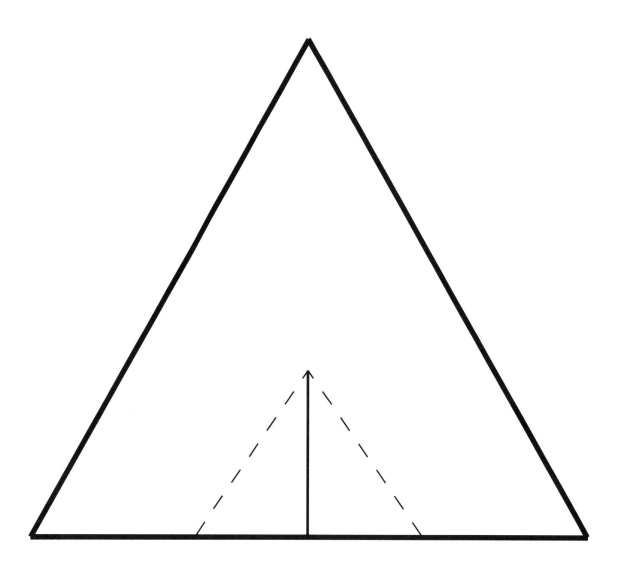

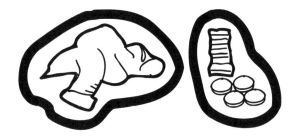

Who Has It?

The children will enjoy making this simple craft, knowing they can play the game with their family.

What You Need

⇨ robe from page 70

⇨ markers

⇨ sequins

⇨ glitter glue pens

⇨ gold ribbon

⇨ scissors

⇨ glue

⇨ craft stick

Before Class

Duplicate the robe from page 70 for each child.

What To Do

1. Give each child a robe to cut out.

2. Instruct the children to decorate the robe.

3. Show how to glue the robe to a craft stick.

To Play

1. Choose one child to be Joshua.

2. Instruct the children to sit on the floor in a circle.

3. The child should walk around the circle, repeating the verse. Then, he or she should drop the robe behind a player, yell "Achan" and run around the circle to see if he or she can sit in "Achan's" place before he is tagged.

4. If Joshua is not tagged, then Achan becomes Joshua and the game is played again.

SAY

How do you think you would have felt if you were Achan? (Allow the children to respond.) Do you think Achan thought his sin was worth the pain and death it caused him and his family? Sin never pays. Follow God's commands to be happy and righteous in Him.

Acceptance

Memory Verse

Do to others as you would have them do to you. ~Luke 6:31

An Enemy Accepted
Based on Acts 9:1-18

The church was under persecution and many had died because they believed in Jesus. One of the prosecutors, Saul, went on a journey to Damascus. Before leaving Jerusalem, he went to see the high priest and received the authority to have anyone arrested who he suspected was a follower of Jesus.

Saul was muttering as he started on his journey. "These Christians! They're taking over. As many as we've persecuted I'd think they would be giving up, but they just seem to be stronger."

Saul shook his head. "Maybe I'll get it stopped in Damascus anyway. I'll arrest everyone I can find and bring them back to Jerusalem where they'll be killed."

Suddenly a light flashed from heaven, knocking Saul off his horse. Saul fell to the ground, hearing a voice saying, "Saul, Saul, why do you hate Me? Why are you hurting Me by hurting My people?"

Saul took a deep breath. "Who are You, Lord?" he asked.

"I am Jesus, the one you are persecuting. When you put My people in prison, you are putting Me in prison. When you kill them, you are killing Me. Now get up and go into the city."

Saul stood, but when he opened his eyes he couldn't see anything. He was blind! His men led him to the place Jesus told him to go. Saul waited in darkness.

In the city lived a man named Ananias. The Lord appeared to him in a vision and said, "Go to Judas' house. When you get there, ask for Saul of Tarsus. Lay hands on him to restore his sight."

"But Lord," protested Ananias. "I know who this man is. He has treated the Christians with hatred and disdain. I have heard he has come to arrest Christians."

"Accept him," commanded the Lord. "I have chosen him to do a great thing for My people."

Ananias obeyed and went to where Saul was staying. "Brother Saul," Ananias said to him. "The Lord sent me to restore your sight so you may be filled with the Holy Ghost."

When Ananias placed his hands over Saul's eyes, sight returned to him. Saul was baptized and immediately began preaching and teaching with the Christians.

For Discussion

Do you have a new boy or girl in your class at school? How would you feel if you were the new one? Should you treat them like you would want to be treated?

Friendship Flags

J oining in the friendship discussion while making these flags will reinforce the lesson of acceptance.

Flag of Friendship

What You Need

⇨ flags from page 73

⇨ craft sticks

⇨ crayons

⇨ glue

⇨ scissors

⇨ gold yarn

Before Class

Duplicate the flags from page 73 for each child. Make a sample flag so the children can see the finished project.

What To Do

1. Give each child a set of flags to color and cut out.

2. Allow the children to glue the flags to the craft sticks.

3. Assist them in tying the yarn around the top of the craft sticks.

SAY

Is it hard to be a friend to someone who has hurt you? (Allow time for discussion.) Give your flag to someone who has hurt you to show that you accept him or her as your friend. Keep the other flag as a reminder of your friendship.

Saul's Horse

Not only will your students have fun making this craft, they will also enjoy using it to retell the Bible story.

What You Need

⇨ story pictures from page 75

⇨ spring-type clothespins

⇨ paper clips

⇨ tape

⇨ glue

⇨ scissors

⇨ markers

Before Class

Duplicate the story pictures from page 75 for each child. Make a sample craft to use in telling the story.

What To Do

1. Give each child a set of story pictures to color and cut out.

2. Instruct the children to clip the clothespins to the horse for legs.

3. Assist in taping the paper clips to the backs of Saul and Ananias so they can interchangedly be attached to the horse.

SAY

Do you think Saul was wicked for persecuting the Christians? (Allow time for students to respond.) Did God still love Saul and give him a chance to become a Christian? Does God still love sinners today?

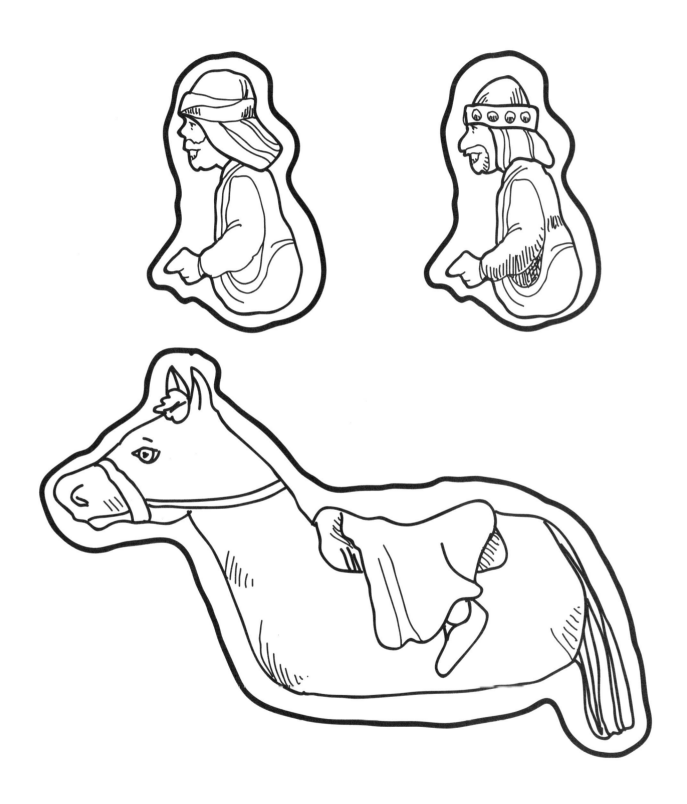

Thriftiness

Memory Verse
The diligent man prizes his possessions.
~Proverbs 12:27

Save the Leftovers
Based on John 6:1-13

Jesus wanted to spend some time away from the crowds that followed Him. He was tired and needed a rest. Jesus, with His 12 disciples, went by boat across the Sea of Galilee. They went to a quiet desert region near Bethsaida.

It didn't take long for the people to find Jesus. Thousands came to see Him and hear Him teach. When Jesus saw their interest, He couldn't turn them away. Jesus spent the day healing the sick and teaching people.

When evening came, one of the disciples said, "You should send the crowds away, Jesus. They must be hungry and they could find food in the nearby villages."

"Why don't we feed them here?" asked Jesus.

"Here?" exclaimed another disciple. "It would take eight months wages to feed all these people! There must be 5,000 men here and that's not counting the women and children."

Andrew had been searching though the crowd, hoping to find some food. He came back to Jesus with a small boy. "This lad has a small lunch. It has five loaves of bread and two small fish. He said You could have it, but it wouldn't go very far."

Jesus told the disciples to have the people sit in groups. Then Jesus gave the boy a hug for his offering. The crowd grew quiet as Jesus lifted up the five loaves and two fish. They listened as He thanked God for giving them something to eat. Then Jesus started breaking up the food. The disciples were amazed at the large baskets He was filling. They started passing them to the people. They ate, and ate and ate.

When everyone was full, Jesus said, "Gather up the leftovers. We should never waste what God has given us."

When the disciples collected the leftovers they had filled twelve baskets! They knew it had been a miracle. And they learned the lesson of thriftiness when they gathered up the remains.

For Discussion

1. How do your treat the possessions you have?

2. Are you careful not to leave them out in the rain? Do you put them where they belong when you are finished with them?

Gather Them Up

Your students can play this game alone or with a friend. As they gather up the leftovers they will be reminded to not waste what they have.

What You Need

⇨ game board and fish from pages 78 and 79

⇨ poster board

⇨ crayons

⇨ glue

⇨ craft sticks

⇨ scissors

⇨ colorful dot stickers

Before Class

Duplicate the game board and fish on pages 78 and 79 on poster board for each child. Make a sample game so you can demonstrate how to play.

What To Do

1. Allow the children to color the fish and cut them out.

2. Instruct the children to cut out the game board. Allow them to put a sticker on each circle.

3. Demonstrate how to glue a craft stick to the back of each side of the game board.

SAY Even though there was enough food to feed all the people, Jesus didn't want to waste the leftovers. See how many fish you can gather. Remember to take care of the things God has given you.

Game Rules

1. Place a fish on every circle except one.

2. Jump one fish over another, making it land on an empty circle. Remove the fish after it has been jumped.

3. Count the number of fish left. The lower the number of the leftovers, the better your score!

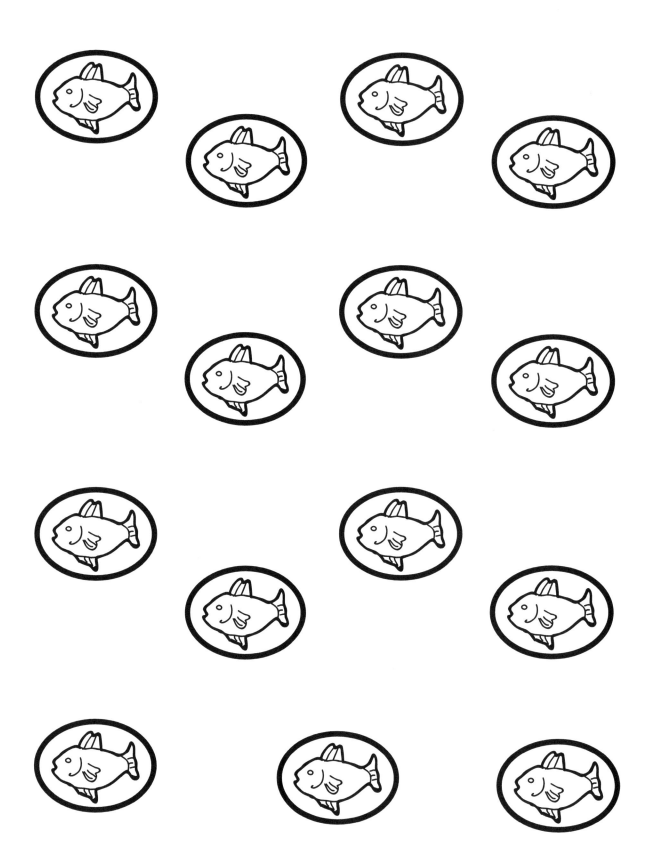

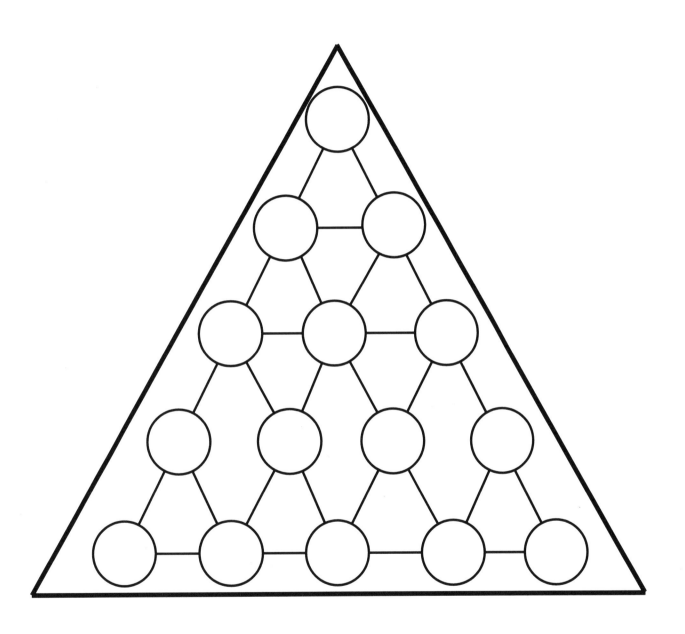

Potato Chip Bag Clip

The children will enjoy making this fun clip and using it will remind them to follow Jesus' example and be thrifty.

What You Need

⇨ boy from page 81

⇨ poster board

⇨ clothespins

⇨ glue

⇨ scissors

⇨ crayons

⇨ small plastic sandwich bags

⇨ potato chips

⇨ permanent marker

Before Class

Duplicate the boy from page 81 on poster board. Fill a plastic bag with potato chips for each child. Make a Potato Chip Bag Clip so the children can see the finished craft.

What To Do

1. Give each child a boy to color and cut out.

2. Instruct the children to glue the boy to the clothespin.

3. Instruct the children to write the memory verse on the other side of clothespin.

4. Give each child a bag of chips. Instruct them to use their clips to keep the chips fresh.

SAY

Do you always remember to close the cereal bag after you use it? What about the chip bag? Being thrifty means making sure you don't let food become stale and inedible. Use your clip to help you be thrifty!

Visiting God

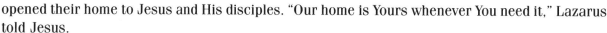

Memory Verse
I will listen to what God the Lord will say.
~Psalm 85:8

Too Busy To Listen
Based on Luke 10:38-42

When Jesus was on earth, He had some special friends. His disciples were His friends, and so were Lazarus and his two sisters, Mary and Martha. The three opened their home to Jesus and His disciples. "Our home is Yours whenever You need it," Lazarus told Jesus.

Jesus enjoyed the peaceful home of Lazarus, Mary and Martha. He visited with them many times to rest from the crowds of people so eager to see Him.

One day, Mary and Martha heard Jesus' familiar knock at their door. They ran to welcome Jesus. After the greeting, Martha hurried to the kitchen to oversee the meal. She wanted everything to be perfect for Jesus. She cleaned every speck of dust her servants had forgotten and gathered herbs for the meal.

Mary, however, never came to assist her. She was so excited about Jesus' being there that she sat as close to His feet as possible and listened to every word He was saying.

Martha started to panic. Would everything be ready in time? The meal would be late! If only Mary would hurry and come help. She could at least get the vegetables from the garden.

Walking swiftly to where Mary was listening to Jesus, Martha interrupted the story He was telling. "Jesus, do You think it is fair that Mary has left me with all the work to do? Will You tell her to come help me?"

Mary's face flushed and she bowed her head. It wasn't that she was too lazy to work, she just wanted to visit with Jesus.

Jesus shook His head at Martha. "Oh, Martha, you are always so busy. It's not important that everything be so perfect. It would be better if you would sit and visit with Me like Mary is."

Martha looked startled, then quickly came over to where Jesus was. "You are right, Jesus. I do need a visit with You." She smiled and sat close to her sister. Together they listened to Him. Martha determined she would never again be too busy to visit with Jesus.

For Discussion

1. Do you like to visit with your friends?

2. Do you think Jesus would like to visit with you? How can you visit together?

Doorknob Hanger

This is a fun craft for your students that will encourage them to find their own special time alone with God.

What You Need

⇨ prayer-time sign and children from page 84

⇨ craft sticks

⇨ yarn

⇨ markers

⇨ glue

⇨ scissors

Before Class

Duplicate the prayer-time sign and children from page 84 for each child. Cut the yarn into 18" pieces. Make a sample Doorknob Hanger so the children can see the finished project.

What To Do

1. Give each student a prayer-time sign and child to color and cut out.

2. Instruct the children to stripe the craft sticks using diagonal lines.

3. Show how to glue the sticks together to form a square.

4. Assist the children in tying the ends of the yarn to one side of the square.

5. Instruct the children to glue the prayer-time sign to the back of the craft sticks.

6. Allow the students to glue the boy or girl to the left side of the words.

SAY

How long do you think our time with God should be each day? (Allow time for students to respond.) God just wants us to spend time with Him each day. So hang this on your doorknob when it's your time to be with God. Your family will know not to bother you while you are talking with your Friend, Jesus.

My Prayer Time

Prayer Reminder

This personalized craft will remind your students to take time for God.

I will listen to what God the Lord will say.
Psalm 85:8
Jason

What You Need

⇨ boy, girl and verse from page 86

⇨ craft sticks

⇨ markers

⇨ glue

⇨ scissors

⇨ small silk flowers (optional)

Before Class

Duplicate boy, girl and verse from page 86 for each child. Make a sample Prayer Reminder so the children can see the finished product.

What To Do

1. Demonstrate how to glue the bottom edge of one craft stick to the back edge of another craft stick. Allow to dry.

2. Give each child a girl or boy and a verse to color and cut out.

3. Instruct the children to sign their names on the line under the verse.

4. If desired, show how to glue some flowers to the bottom craft stick.

SAY We have so many distractions to keep us from finding time to talk and listen to God. Can you tell me some of them? (Allow time for student response.) Let's keep our pledge to take time for God.

I will
listen to
what God
the Lord
will say.

Psalm 85:8

_____

Resisting Temptation

Memory Verse

When you are tempted, he will also provide a way out so that you can stand up under it. ~1 Corinthians 10:13

No Way!
Based on Genesis 37 & 39

Joseph's brothers hated him. The brothers were jealous of the love their father, Jacob, had for Joseph. One day when Joseph had been sent to check on his brothers they seized him and sold him to a group of Ishmaelites. The Ishmaelites were on their way to Egypt with camels loaded with things to sell.

When Joseph arrived in Egypt with the Ishmaelites they sold him to one of Pharoah's officers, Potiphar. Potiphar was captain of the guard.

It wasn't long until Potiphar realized he had bought a good slave. Joseph was very skillful, but best of all he was willing to work hard. Potiphar made Joseph head of his household.

Joseph was young and good-looking. All of those who saw him were impressed. One of these was Potiphar's wife. Time after time, she tried to tempt him.

"Come, Joseph, spend some time with me."

But Joseph always had the same answer. "No way, wife of Potiphar. Your husband trusts me and I will not do what is wrong in his eyes and in the eyes of my God."

Day after day, Potiphar's wife waited for Joseph to come into view. Day after day, she begged him to stay with her. Day after day, Joseph repeated his answer, "No way."

One day Joseph got too close to the wife of his master. Potiphar's wife grabbed hold of the sleeve of his coat. Quickly, Joseph slipped his arm out of the sleeve and made his escape, leaving the woman with nothing but his coat.

"Help!" she cried, calling the servants. "Look what that Hebrew, Joseph, tried to do!" Potiphar's wife held up Joseph's coat. "He tried to hurt me, but when I yelled he ran away, leaving this behind."

As soon as Potiphar came home she told him the same lies. Enraged that a servant would touch his wife, he had Joseph thrown in prison.

As Joseph sat in the dark, damp prison he thought, *I'm still glad I resisted temptation and said, "No way." My heart is clean before God regardless of the result. He will care for me here.*

For Discussion

What is your biggest temptation? Can you resist it by yourself?

Joseph's Robes Game

Decorating the robes for this game will be fun for your students. Playing the game will be, too!

What You Need

⇨ robes and "P" from page 89

⇨ spring-type clothespins

⇨ markers

⇨ scissors

Before Class

Duplicate the robes and "P" from page 89 onto poster board for each child. Make a sample game so you can play with your students if there is an uneven number.

What To Do

1. Give each child the duplicated robes to decorate.

2. Instruct the children to cut out the robes and the "P."

3. Allow the children to clip a clothespin to the bottom of each robe.

4. Explain the rules of the game: Choose a partner.

Set your robes up facing your partner.

One partner will hide his or her head while the other clips the "P" behind one of the robes.

The partner then tries to guess which robe is hiding the "P." If he or she guesses correctly, the hider must say the memory verse. If he or she guesses incorrectly, that player says the verse. A point is added to the score of the one who says the verse.

Continue to take turns for 10 rounds. The one with the least amount of points wins.

SAY

Potiphar's wife tried to trick Joseph into sinning. Has anyone ever tried to trick you into doing wrong? (Allow time for the students to respond.) The devil is quick to whisper temptations into your ear, but be like Joseph and say, "No way!"

Pocket Pal

Your students will enjoy using their creativity to produce a one-of-a-kind Pocket Pal.

What You Need

⇨ Pocket Pal from page 91

⇨ scissors

⇨ crayons

⇨ wiggle eyes

⇨ yarn

⇨ scissors

⇨ ribbon

⇨ felt

⇨ craft sticks

⇨ tape

Before Class

Duplicate the pocket pal from page 91 on poster board. Make a sample Pocket Pal to wear while welcoming your students to class.

What To Do

1. Give each child a Pocket Pal to cut out.

2. Instruct the children to use their imaginations to color and create a one-of-a-kind Pocket Pal.

3. Assist the children in taping the Pocket Pal to the top of a craft stick.

4. Show how to slip the bottom of the stick into a pocket to wear the pal. Suggest the children can also insert the Pocket Pal on a book, calendar or backpack pocket.

SAY

Each of our Pocket Pals are different, just like we are all different. (Logan) you have straight blond hair, and (Brittany) you have brown curly hair. (William's) eyes are blue and (Allison's) eyes are brown. Just like we are different, the devil tempts us all with different things. He might tempt you to ignore your mother's bedtime rule, or you might be tempted to steal a pack of gum from the store. Remember Joseph and run from temptation!

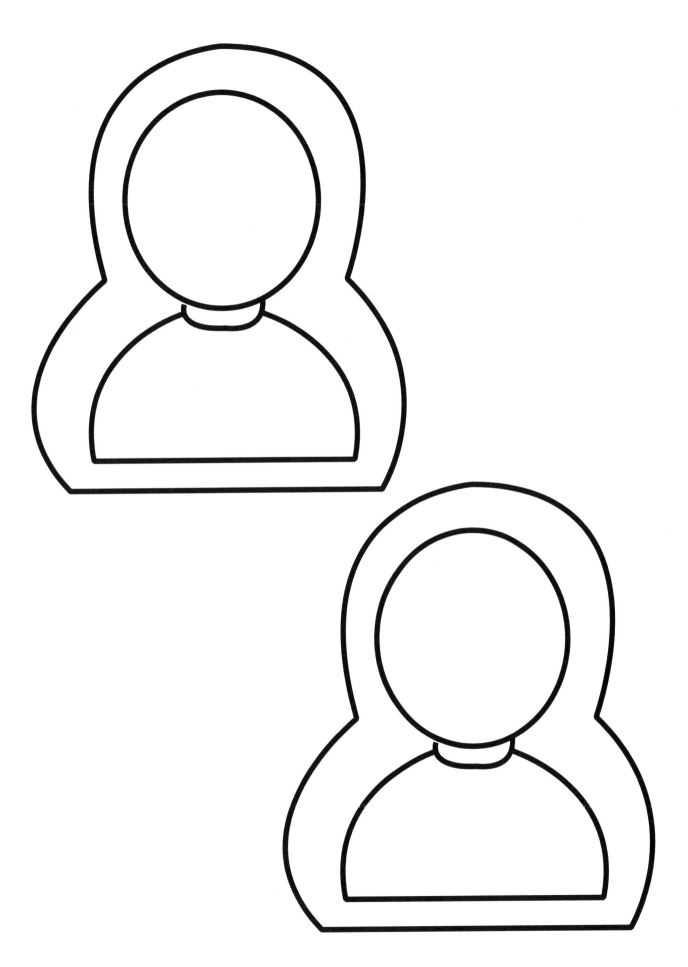

Riches

Memory Verse

What good will it be for a man if he gains the whole world, yet forfeits his soul. ~Matthew 16:26

I Love My Money
Based on Mark 10

A young man came running up to Jesus and knelt before Him. Jesus could tell by looking at him that he came from a wealthy family.

"Lord, what can I do so that I can have eternal life? I want to live forever," said the young man.

"You should keep all the commandments," answered Jesus.

The young man looked up into the face of Jesus. "I have kept all the commandments since I was a young boy."

Jesus knew that this young man's money and the things it had bought were very important to him. So Jesus said, "If you want to live forever in heaven, take all your possessions and sell them. Then give your money to the poor. Then God will be the most important thing in your life and you can enter heaven."

The young man slowly got to his feet. His eyes were sad as he looked at Jesus. He couldn't give up all he had. He wanted to keep his things in first place in his heart and give God second place.

As the young man walked away, Jesus asked His disciples, "How big is the eye of the needle?"

They were surprised at the question. "Very tiny," one answered. "Just small enough for a thread to go through."

"It would be easier for a camel to go through an eye of an needle than for a rich man to enter into heaven," Jesus told them.

The disciples knew what Jesus was saying. Having money was not wrong, but it was wrong for those who put it first in their lives.

For Discussion

1. What is your most prized possession?

2. Is it worth more to you than getting to heaven?

Bell Pull Reminder

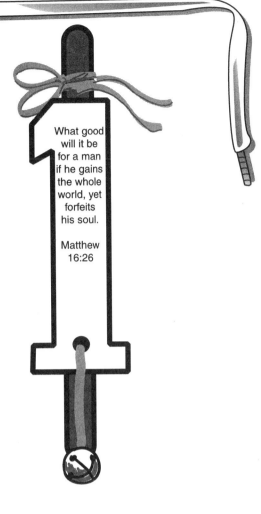

What good will it be for a man if he gains the whole world, yet forfeits his soul.

Matthew 16:26

Every time your students hear the bell from this craft they will be reminded to keep Jesus first.

What You Need

⇨ number 1 from page 94

⇨ colored poster board

⇨ craft sticks

⇨ yarn

⇨ jingle bells

⇨ glue

⇨ scissors

⇨ hole punch

⇨ markers

Before Class

Duplicate the large number 1 from page 94 to colored poster board for each child. Make a sample Bell Pull to hang on your classroom door.

What To Do

1. Give each child a number 1 to cut out.

2. Instruct the children to glue a craft stick to the back of the 1.

3. Assist the children in tying yarn to the end of the craft stick for a hanger.

4. Allow the children to punch a hole on the bottom of the number 1 where indicated.

5. Assist the children in tying a jingle bell to the number 1 with yarn, allowing a space between the number and the bell. Tie the ends of the yarn in a bow.

6. Have the students write the memory verse on the 1.

SAY

The rich young man wanted to put his money before Jesus and still get to heaven. Is money sinful? No, it is only sinful when it becomes more important than God. So be careful of your possessions. Keep Jesus #1!

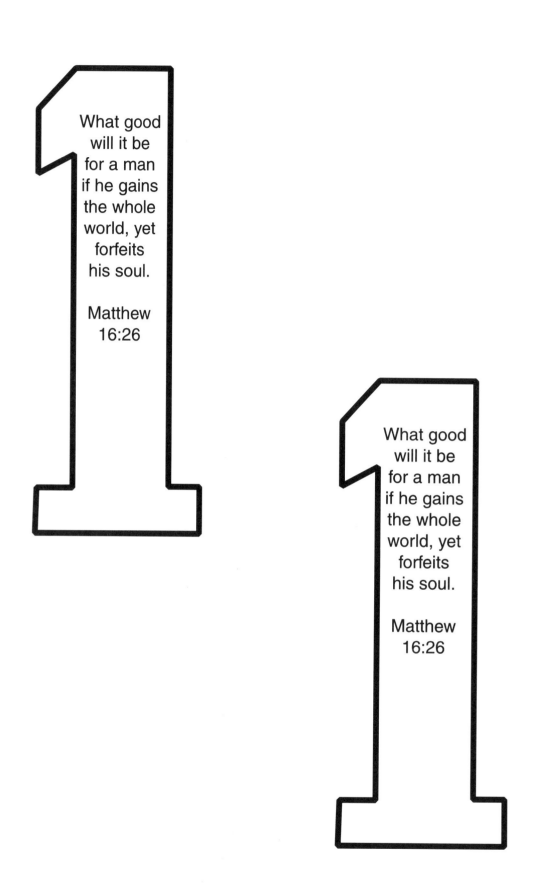

What good
will it be
for a man
if he gains
the whole
world, yet
forfeits
his soul.

Matthew
16:26

What good
will it be
for a man
if he gains
the whole
world, yet
forfeits
his soul.

Matthew
16:26

Change Holder

This Pocket Change Holder is fun to make and fun to use.

What good will it be for a man if he gains the whole world, yet forfeits his soul.   Matthew 16:26

What You Need

⇨ verse square from page 96

⇨ craft sticks

⇨ hairspray can lids

⇨ scissors

⇨ glue

⇨ small stickers of Jesus

Before Class

Duplicate the verse square from page 96 for each child. Make a sample Pocket Change Holder so the children can see the finished project.

What To Do

1. Give each child a verse square to color and cut out.

2. Instruct each child to glue craft sticks together to form a square.

3. Have the students glue the square the back of the craft sticks.

4. Allow the children to glue a lid on the square.

5. Give the children stickers of Jesus to place in the square and encourage them to draw hearts around Jesus.

SAY

This Change Holder will be a good place for you to keep your money. When you see Jesus inside the hearts, remember the rich, young man who came to see Jesus. Keep Jesus first in your heart.

What good will it be for a man
if he gains the whole world, yet
forfeits his soul.   Matthew 16:26

What good will it be for a man
if he gains the whole world, yet
forfeits his soul.   Matthew 16:26